# The Parents' Guide to Raising a Lacrosse Player:

## A Mental Health Approach

Published by Salt Water Media
29 Broad Street, Suite 104
Berlin, MD 21811
www.saltwatermedia.com

*Salt Water*
M E D I A

Cover art used with license from istockphoto.com
Author photo provided by the author
Interior graphics used with license from istockphoto.com

# The Parents' Guide to Raising a Lacrosse Player:

## A Mental Health Approach

Erica M. Dixon
LCPC, LCADC

**To dad** – My Renaissance Man.


**To my clients** – Thank you for entrusting me with your stories. I am deeply honored and have learned so much from all of you. Your presence in my life has made me a better therapist.

*All client names have been changed to protect their confidentiality.*

# Contents

# Introduction
# The Club Scene

It's 5:00 a.m. and your alarm blares. You drag yourself out of bed because you have to get the cooler and lunches ready for the day. You pack up the car, stacking folding chairs, cooling towels, and, of course, plenty of water and extra ice. You cannot forget the Advil and knee brace, just in case. Does she have her stick, goggles and mouth guard? Shoot, I have to remind her to bring both jerseys. It takes an hour to get to the sports complex and another twenty minutes to find a parking space. Why is the first game always so damn early? What field is the team on, anyway? Where should I park if she plays on a different field for each game? Where is my coffee? Much like a sherpa, you heft the chairs, cooler, and all of the supplies to the field to watch your daughter play four games in sweltering July heat.

❌ ❌ ❌

It's a cool and sunny October afternoon. The teams are warming up on opposite ends of the field. Parents and students sit on the bleachers chatting and talking strategy. The scoreboard is lit and the announcer tests his microphone. Everyone stands for the national anthem. The opening whistle blows, and the game begins. As the game clock counts down, parents become more vocal, gawking at missteps and shouting dissent at the referees. When the game ends, a father walks alongside his son asking about certain plays and what he could have done better.

YOUR SON'S TEAM MAKES IT TO THE youth championship. The cheering crowd is on its feet as the game goes into overtime. It is awe-inspiring how hard the boys play for one another. You see them lift each other up and keep the motivation high. Your son makes the winning shot. *Victory!* It is exhilarating to watch the boys dogpile each other. Pride swells in your chest and you wipe a tear away watching how your son's team laughs, cheers, and hugs one another. After the game, you hear a father from the other team screaming at his son. The father makes his son run sprints on the field with push-ups in between in order to teach him a lesson. Parents stop to stare at the boy who is now audibly crying. You gather your son from the locker room, wrapping your arm around his shoulders. On the field, the other father is still yelling obscenities.

RAISING AN ATHLETE TAKES TIME AND COMMITMENT, but it affects parents emotionally as well. I have seen a wide range of parental emotions and behaviors. Some are positive in nature, and some are downright abusive.

I have been lucky to raise two athletes of my own: two strong, kind, hard-working, undeniably resilient lacrosse players. I am also a licensed clinician with experience treating a wide variety of mental health issues over the past three decades. Many of my clients were lacrosse players, themselves, who sought help for a number of reasons related to the sport. Some of their stories will be highlighted in the vignettes in the coming chapters. But first, let's develop a foundation in therapy.

What makes us act in certain ways and not others? The short answer is **how we think.** Examining the history of Cognitive Behavioral Therapy will help us understand more.

Cognitive Behavioral Therapy gradually evolved from behavioral practices. Behaviorism is the theory that behaviors are acquired through conditioning. Growing up, we all probably learned about Ivan Pavlov and his famous dogs. Pavlov's discovery that the dogs' automatic salivation (a subconscious or automatic response) to food (an unconditioned stimulus) could be further developed and trained. Over the course of his experiments, the dogs learned that every time a bell would ring it meant he would receive a treat. The dogs soon grew so conditioned that they would begin salivating when they heard the bell, whether or not food was forthcoming.

In the 1920s, John B. Watson continued this research of classical conditioning but applied it to humans. In Watson and Raynor's classic study involving a 9-month-old child named Albert, the researchers paired an unconditioned stimulus that automatically elicited fear (the sound of a hammer hitting a metal bar) with a rat. Little Albert associated the sound of the hammer with the rat and became fearful of the rat. The researchers then paired the fear stimulus with a rabbit and a dog. Little Albert became fearful of both of these animals as well. While this particular experiment taught researchers a lot, I know it goes without saying that you shouldn't try this at home.

Psychologists continued to believe in the importance of behaviors and disregarded the importance of the role cognitions play. In the 1940s, B.F. Skinner developed the theory of Operant Conditioning which was a theory of how we learn. This theory examined the causes of an action and its subsequent consequences. The terms of positive reinforcement, negative reinforcement, and punishment were introduced. Positive reinforcement increases the chances of a particular behavior reoccurring by pairing the behavior with a pleasant stimulus, such as Pavlov's dogs receiving a treat. Negative reinforcement increases the chances of a behavior occurring when the stimulus is removed, such as turning off an annoying alarm clock, so you'll get out of bed. Punishment decreases the frequency of a behavior by introducing a negative consequence, such as taking away your teen's iPhone after breaking curfew.

In the 1950s, Dr. Albert Ellis explored how thoughts played a role with Operant Conditioning. This idea led to his practice of Rational Emotive Behavior Therapy. His goal was to help patients change their behaviors and change how they felt by identifying their irrational or unhelpful thoughts. (I had the pleasure of taking a seminar with him. He was amazing and cursed like a sailor.)

Another step toward the discovery of Cognitive Behavioral Therapy occurred in the 1960s, at the University of Pennsylvania. Dr. Aaron T. Beck noticed that the depressed patients he was treating often had automatic negative thinking. He developed the Beck Depression Inventory and the Beck Anxiety Inventory. Dr. Beck worked with his patients to change their negative self-talk and replace it with more reasonable self-talk. He found that in doing so, his patients began to feel better. Dr. Beck is thought of as the founder of Cognitive Behavioral Therapy.

After Dr. Beck's foundational work in Cognitive Behavioral Therapy, Dr. David Burns, a student of Dr. Beck's in the 1970s, went on to revolutionize the field in his breakthrough book, *The Feeling Good Handbook*. His work teaches readers how to overcome their negative thinking in order to feel better. Dr. Burns' ongoing clinical work and research has made Cognitive Behavioral Therapy one of the most popular and sought after modes of treatment.

I teach all of my clients about CBT and how they can replace their automatic negative thoughts with more reasonable and believable ones in order to improve mood. I believe that thoughts lead to feelings which lead to behaviors. The next chapters examine several case studies of emotionally charged situations with different athletes and how CBT can be utilized to work through them. My greatest hope is that readers of this book gain strategies and talking points that positively impact the way they interact with their student athlete. There will likely be challenges you and your athlete face, but with these strategies, concepts, and talking points in mind, I hope that you will be able to communicate openly, and honestly, and together overcome these obstacles.

# Self-Doubt

## Part 1: The Basics

Losing faith in your abilities can be devastating. A lack of confidence in yourself and your abilities can have a rippling effect on every facet of life, but when young athletes are involved, self-doubt has a way of impacting one of their greatest passions: their sport. Self-confidence, and its opposite of self-doubt, can make or break an athlete's performance. One of my former teammates used to say that lacrosse is 10% athletic ability and 90% mental toughness. Student athletes who cycle into self-doubt often make poor decisions on the field, put in less effort, and struggle to cope with the pressure of practices and games. When athletes tell themselves that they are not good enough or saying "I can't" will undoubtedly cause a negative performance.

Self-Doubt can manifest in a variety of ways including:

| | |
|---|---|
| Poor decision-making | Athletes may hesitate, play it safe, be more risk avoidant which can ultimately hinder performance. They are not "playing hard" because they doubt themselves. |

| Poor concentration | Athletes may worry about mistakes they haven't even made yet, which impacts their ability to react in the moment. They may be thinking about making a mistake and forget to catch the ball or forget the play that the coach called out. |
|---|---|
| Perfectionism | Athletes may strive for flawless performances and be overly critical of any perceived failings. |
| Anxiety/Depression | Games and even practices can be stressful. A flare up in Anxiety can occur; chronic anxiety can also lead to depression. |
| Imposter Syndrome | Athletes who fear that they aren't as skilled as their teammates may develop worry over being "exposed" as a fraud. |
| Burnout | Athletes may become so emotionally and physically exhausted in managing their self-doubt, among other pressures, that they lose interest in their sport. |

During his work, Dr. Burns formulated mood surveys which you can find in any of his books such as his latest, *Feeling Great: The Revolutionary New Treatment for Depression and Anxiety.* These surveys aim to assess a patient's levels of depression, anxiety, anger and other factors. These tools are used by mental health professionals to evaluate the severity of these complex emotions for tracking and treatment purposes. However, parents or caregivers can use them if they believe that their athlete is slipping into a cycle of self-doubt. Recognizing those signs and working to alleviate them early on helps your child access the vocabulary and reflectiveness to talk about why they feel the way they do. Remember, thoughts lead to feelings which lead to behaviors. If your athlete can verbalize how he or she feels, he or she can take steps to change these thoughts which will lead to a change in behaviors.

## Part 2: The Case Study

Jack came to my practice as a freshman in high school. He had been playing club lacrosse since the age of six. He was regarded by most of his peers as a high-caliber player. However, Jack was devastated when he did not make the varsity team his freshman year. He began to doubt his ability to play in high school and college. More devastating to Jack, his parents seemed to doubt his athletic ability as well. He started to lose motivation in junior varsity practice, but his grades remained high, and he continued being involved in all his social engagements.

The first thing I wanted to evaluate was Jack's mood. Was he anxious? Depressed? The Burns Brief Mood survey was used to obtain an accurate gauge on overall mood.

Mood surveys are a great way to collect data. It is also good to keep the results, so you have something to compare it to later. I realize that getting a teenager to take a mood survey may be like extracting a tooth from a rhinoceros but do your best. Use a compassionate approach. Let your child know that you are worried about him or her and this is a way that he/she can communicate with you without having to say a word!

In this case, Jack scored a 10 on the Depression Scale, a 6 on the Anxiety Scale, 0 on Suicidality, and 4 on Anger. In other words, he was mildly to moderately depressed and feeling badly about himself but denied suicidal ideation. The score was consistent with his behaviors. During our sessions, Jack shared that he was doing well in school but lost motivation for his sport. His overall mood was down, and he no longer believed in his ability to do well. The important distinction was that while he doubted his ability to do well, this sentiment didn't translate to all aspects of his life. It was centered around lacrosse only.

So, what do we do now? In cases like this, I like to introduce a handout, entitled "Cognitive Distortions." It is a list of ten ways that we tend to be irrational in our thinking. It is important to know that we *all* have moments of cognitive distortions; it is completely normal at any age. No one gets through life being completely rational *all* the time.

This list of 10 Cognitive Distortions can easily be found online or again, in any of Dr. Burns' books. When a person uses one or more of these distortions, without the added rationale to understand that it's a distortion, he or she can run into some trouble. What we *think*, determines how we *feel*, and then that determines how we *behave*. Once we understand when and how we are distorting our thinking, we can take steps to change it. The distorted thought is called an automatic negative thought. It just pops in our head without much awareness.

For instance, Jack's automatic negative response when asked about his favorite sport was, "I am not a good lacrosse player." He believed this to be very true even though he experienced significant success on the field prior to getting cut from varsity. This thought made him feel insecure and sad. He then did not put forth effort in practice since he was unmotivated.

It became a self-fulfilling prophecy. The narrative cycled over and over again: *I am not that good at this, so I am not going to try so hard in practice since it won't make a difference anyway.*

The first thing I wanted to do was point out the distortions in Jack's thinking. Jack was using **all or nothing thinking** because his statement was very black and white. However, we all know that being good or bad at something does not always necessitate the crisis that we make it. Jack was also using **labeling** in his thought process. He was putting himself down and creating a vicious cycle of shame. Once Jack could see the distortions in his thinking, he could put in the work to correct it. If your child is going through something similar to Jack, ask him or her to come up with what's known as a "replacement thought."

The triple column handout, developed by Dr. Burns, can help with this process. Simply identify the negative thought in the first column. Identify which distortions you may be using in that thought and write them in the second column. Then, in the third and last column, write in a replacement thought that is believable to you. This replacement thought has to be believable and reasonable otherwise, the exercise will not be impactful. Jack was able to come up with *"I have been a good player since I was six years old. I have learned valuable skills but now I am being challenged."* Coming up with this was excellent progress for Jack. He was able to recognize that he is a good player and that being challenged at his sport meant that he had room to improve and get even better. Jack asked his parents if they would be willing to hire a shooting coach for extra help. By facing his challenge head-on, overcoming his distorted thinking, and creating a positive replacement thought, he was able to create a plan with his parents to continue improving.

The other skill that was an important tool in Jack's toolbox was imagery. I asked Jack to breathe deeply and watch himself walk onto the field, feeling relaxed and confident. I asked Jack to watch himself warm up, and play his position effectively and skillfully, making his shots at all different angles. Jack was able to do this in a relaxed manner that gave him confidence on the field.

After four weeks, I asked Jack to take the Burns Depression and Anxiety Inventory again. His scores were 5 and 3 respectively, and a 0 on Suicidality and a 0 on Anger, a big improvement from his first assessment.

Jack's parents had to make a few adjustments as well. They could not approach Jack if they were also feeling insecure and anxious about their son's performance. They needed to do the same exercises in order to gain a more objective perspective. A parent conveys messages even when they do not verbalize their words. Jack needed to know that his performance on the field had nothing to do with how they felt about him. Jacks' parents were able to separate the athletic performance from who their son was as a person. Once these adjustments were made, Jack felt more secure and guess what – started performing better.

**Part 3: What Parents Can Do**

1. Administer a mood survey to get an idea of how your athlete is feeling, especially if he or she won't tell you on their own.

2. Talk with your child about the results. Reassure him or her that these feelings are normal to have. Say things like "We can grow from it. It does not have to keep us stuck in a negative place."

3. Teach him or her about the cognitive distortions and how to change the negative thoughts. This is an easy way to change your thinking so we can change the way you feel.

4. Examine your own negative thoughts about the situation. It's important for parents to be supportive of their child. Are you expecting too much? Putting too much pressure on your child? Are you making his or her lacrosse performance more important than it needs to be?

# Adjusting to College Level Lacrosse

## Part 1: The Basics

The real work starts in college. The transition from high school sports to Division 1 is significant and often overwhelming. Many students find that they have to work harder than they ever needed to before, not just at their sport but at the academic expectations, too. Athletes have to balance their time more than ever. Athletes have to make more sacrifices. The emotional and physical drain on a collegiate level athlete is significant and high school rarely prepares you for it.

I think it is important to talk about the experience, so more athletes know what to expect. Playing a division 1 sport is one of the most challenging experiences a young person can choose to do.

## Part 2: The Case Study

When David got to college to play lacrosse, he noticed a few changes immediately. His time was dictated by school and his sport. He rarely had free time. His day started at 8:00 a.m., and ended at 9:00 p.m. The day consisted of morning practice, watching film, attending class, eating with his team, homework and studying and checking into study hall. David is an extrovert on the Myers Briggs type indicator, but he also likes and needs his time alone to recharge. He had to make a few choices. He chose not to go out as much as some of his teammates so he could study. He also chose to study in the team lounge where he could be alone. The balance was a bit tricky at first, but David found a good one for himself.

The second challenge was being on the scout team. He, of course, was always a starter so this transition was very frustrating. The scout team is the practice squad for those players who will get time in a game. They mimic players from the opposing team to get the starters ready to play against them. David worked very hard to try to get noticed by the coaches. Obviously, he wanted as much playing time as possible.

He ended up getting upset and frustrated because he was not producing. The coach noticed this and told him that he was forcing it and trying to do too much. However, David was not sure how to change it. He came to me for a few sessions, and we worked on changing his thinking so he could improve his mood and thus change his behaviors on the field.

We started with identifying his automatic negative thoughts. David told himself for weeks that "I must make a big play every time I have the ball." This ended up being too much pressure on himself and he ended up forcing plays that were ill advised and resulted in a turnover.

Instead, we talked about "make the next smart, small play." We also talked about slowing down his thoughts and being more present in the play.

"Catch the ball first" was always step one.

Step two was, "Now, make the next smart, small play."

He and his coach talked about this as well. Many small

plays will grow into big plays. David had to work up to that. He also had to accept that this is where his thoughts were at this point in time. He could not ignore them because they were changing his mood and behaviors. He had to notice his thoughts and accept them and then work on changing them.

This worked well for David. It also helped that his coach was knowledgeable about cognitive behavioral therapy and reinforced the replacement thoughts for David.

The second challenge was the fear of making a mistake. His thoughts were: "It will be awful if I make a mistake" or "I could get pulled from the game or lose an opportunity."

Unfortunately, these thoughts are somewhat rational. It can be awful when a player (who is trying to prove himself) makes a mistake. Most coaches will pull the player, and he may not get another opportunity for that game.[1] If this rationale were a consistent coaching strategy for all players on the field, then it may be beneficial to the team. However, when it is a coaching rationale for some and not for others, it is demoralizing.

This is also a ridiculous coaching rationale at the younger ages. All children who are playing a sport should be developed. This should be a mandatory coaching rationale below the high school age groups.

So, what did David do with his fears? He could not allow himself to continue to think this way and let his fear paralyze

---

1 Note: This exists at all levels of the game from elementary age on up to college. Wherever your athlete is on the spectrum, remember that this is a battle they may encounter. Knowing how to recognize the need for some cognitive behavioral therapy when things happen outside of your child's control is an important step in helping them grow not just as an athlete, but as a person.

his performance. We came up with a few strategies that worked well.

Using the replacement thought "I can only control myself" and "I will play and think to the best of my ability" helped combat some of the negative self-talk he'd been replaying in his mind.

1.  He was encouraged to take a few deep breaths to clear his mind. Only focus on your inhale and exhale for a few minutes. Let your thoughts move to the background.

2.  Then, he was encouraged to "make the next smart, small play."

3.  We also used visualization techniques so he could see himself make the next smart play while breathing deeply and relaxing.

4.  In this situation, David was also able to have a conversation with his coach. This is a helpful tool, and the coach actually admitted that he needs to work on his own patience with his non-starters.

## Part 3: What Parents Can Do

1.  Ask your player about the sport-life balance he or she is adapting and how it is working for him or her.

2.  Ask your player about how he or she is feeling about practice. Don't ask her how many draws she won or how many goals she scored. We don't want to link these variables to her rate of success. Instead, get her perspective on it and reinforce her for whatever insights she presents. For example, "it sounds like you have a lot of

insight into how you are playing. Self-reflection is so important as an athlete." Another example, "I am so happy to hear you self-reflect and not self-criticize!"

3.  Offer questions that allow your athlete to reflect on his or her behavior and self-talk, if you notice that he or she is being too hard on herself. One suggestion to start might be, "It sounds like you are criticizing yourself pretty harshly. Is that helpful to you?"

# For Parents

Just as challenging as it is for players, it is equally difficult for you, the parents. I call it the Division 1 Woes. It is so exciting for your child to be recruited to play a Division 1 college sport. However, the emotional and physical work starts here for the parents and the player. Most often, the brutal let down of watching your child on the bench is the disappointing aftermath of this recruiting process. You may be used to watching your child play for the majority of every single game. He or she was the star – one of the best on the field.

How does a parent cope with watching their child play consistently and then watching their college team play without him or her even touching the field? You may get angry or sad or frustrated. What are your thoughts about it? Examine them now. I encourage you to write them down.

Perhaps you think: "This is awful. My child is working so hard in practice. Is #14 really that much better?"

"Why does he get to play and my kid doesn't?"

"Is she ever going to see the field?"

"Maybe committing to this school was a mistake."

"My child is never going to be happy if he or she is not playing."

"It's terrible that my child never lived up to his/her potential as a player."

"Maybe my athlete is just not working hard enough."

"What does the coach have against him or her?"

What if —and here is a safe space to admit it – you think that no matter how much you love your child, "How can I be proud of him if he is not the star on the field?"

Do these thoughts resonate? Do they sound irrational?

Even though your child is wrapped up in being an athlete, remember that it is not their entire identity. There is more to your child and your love for them cannot be conditional on their performance on the field. No matter how much playing time your child gets at the college level, remember to be proud of him or her for having a positive attitude, staying diligent, and working hard in the classroom as well as on the practice field.

If you are having any of the above irrational thoughts, I challenge you to replace them with a thought that is reasonable, rational and believable to you.

AS SEEN IN THE PREVIOUS CHAPTER, IT is a helpful tool for your player as well. Using strategies like the triple column can be extremely beneficial in sorting and diffusing some of our most upsetting thoughts. Remember, too, that doing activities like this for yourself allow you the mental space and energy that your athlete will need from you. They need your support more than anything else, and so the responsibility of maintaining your own mental health has multi-faceted benefits.

A good friend of mine says playing a collegiate sport is a

journey we all take together. None of us are experiencing this in a bubble. It is hard to watch a college team compete while your son or daughter is standing on the sidelines. At the end of the game, there may be a small pit in your stomach due to some of the above negative thinking. Remember that what we think determines how we feel and that in turn, determines our behaviors.

If we think, *"it is devastating that she did not play."* Then, it leads us to feeling sad, hopeless, and frustrated. Our behaviors follow this path. We may yell at a loved one or mouth off to some of the parents on the team. We may just isolate ourselves. Remember that if you are feeling and thinking this way, there is a good chance that another team parent can relate.

According to the NCAA, statistically 3.3% of male high school lacrosse players go on to play Division 1. 4.3% of female high school lacrosse players go on to Division 1. These statistics are similar for other sports. From there, a small percentage of those athletes see the field with consistency.

Historically, sports have been around since the first civilization and athletes have a long history of being glorified. Lacrosse has a different history. Lacrosse is the oldest team sport in North America. The Creator's Game, as it was originally called by the indigenous tribes that invented it, was spiritual in nature. One story of the game's origin tells us that Sky Woman fell from the Heavens and landed on the great turtle's back. Sky Woman rubbed soil on the turtle's back and it became Earth.

Sky Woman had a daughter named Tekawerahkwa or Breath of the Wind. She gave birth to twins who did not get along. One twin was Sapling who had a normal birth. The other twin was Flint who was born out of Breath of the Wind's armpit, thus killing her in childbirth. Sky Woman raised the twins and taught them how to play lacrosse in order to peacefully resolve their constant disputes.

Particularly for the Iroquois tribe, Haudenosaunee, the Creator's Game is a way to channel aggression without becoming violent. Most indigenous tribes will say that lacrosse has healing and medicinal powers. In times of sickness, healers would call on Mother Earth to help them choose the right medicines. The healers would often request a game of lacrosse to be played in order to improve the power of these medicines. The Creators game promoted wellness and community. Lacrosse was originally meant to be something that transcends the glorification of being an athlete.

I wonder if this mindset can lend some perspective.

# Depression

Depression is a common and potentially serious mental health condition that affects millions of people. It's often characterized by persistent feelings of sadness and loss of interest in activities that used to bring joy (anhedonia). People with serious cases of depression often withdraw from people and places that they usually interact with; sometimes major depressive disorders can affect a person so severely that they have trouble engaging in life. There are additional symptoms of depression listed below. While no single item on the list indicates depression 100% of the time, it's worth paying attention for these symptoms and whether they increase disproportionately over time. It may indicate the need for further conversations and/or mental health treatment for your athlete.

## Symptoms of Depression

- Disproportionate sadness, feeling empty, or irritability
- Anhedonia – markedly diminished interest in activities
- Significant weight loss or weight gain
- Persistent Insomnia or hypersomnia
- Feeling restless or feeling very sluggish

- Consistent Fatigue
- Decreased ability to think or concentrate
- Increased indecisiveness
- Feelings of worthlessness or hopelessness or excessive guilt
- Thoughts of suicide

According to the 5th text revised edition of the *Diagnostic and Statistical Manual (DSM) of Mental Disorders*, there are eight kinds of depressive disorders. When looking at Major Depressive Disorder, specifically, five or more of these symptoms have to be present for at least two weeks before warranting a diagnosis and one of those symptoms has to be depressed/sad mood or anhedonia. These symptoms obviously cause significant disruption in the person's daily life. There are many reasons why an athlete can experience a depressive episode. It can be related to injury or illness or not performing well. But it can also be due to a romantic breakup, conflicts with friends, family issues or a genetic predisposition.

**Part 2: The Case Study**

Like so many athletes, Peter fell in love with his sport at an early age. He was driven to learn and became obsessed with all things lacrosse. However, he grew up in an area of the country where lacrosse was not a popular sport, so his parents drove hours in order for Pete to join competitive teams. All Peter wanted to do was play with the best team and best coaches he could find. He was highly motivated, and his goal was to play for a Division 1 university.

Peter was so talented; he made varsity during his freshman year of high school. Peter's schedule was a full day of school and then practice with his team for two hours. After practice, his mom picked him up and they drove home where their family of six ate dinner at all hours of the evening. Pete would complete his homework and often went back outside to do wall ball drills or agility drills for an additional hour.

He taught himself how to string lacrosse sticks and started a small business venture before getting a job at a local sports equipment store where he was able to string sticks for athletes in the area.

Pete did well during the school year, earning accolades in his county and getting noticed by college coaches. During the summer months, Pete played for the best club team he could find (within a reasonable driving distance). In fact, Peter's skill was so advanced that many of the area club coaches reached out to the family to personally invite Pete to play for them.

Suffice it to say, Pete ate, slept and breathed lacrosse. He was fully committed to the sport that he loved. His parents agreed to the excessive driving to notable clubs because they wanted their son to have the best chances of achieving his dream of playing Division 1.

In the fall of his junior year of high school, Peter was recruited by a number of colleges and universities. He was thoughtful about the process, meeting with each coach and staff, touring the school and matching his academic interests with the programs the school offered. He wrote thank you letters to each coach and kept in contact with each of them as he made his decision. Pete chose to play for a university in his home state. He was thrilled with his decision and so was his family. Pete felt supported by his college coach and was told that the expectation was for him to start as a long stick defensive midfielder.

With his dreams and expectations soaring, it seemed like there was no stopping Peter.

Until a devastating injury altered the course of Peter's life. During his freshman year of college, during the first contact practice of the season, Pete tore his ACL and meniscus.

It was a devastating injury, resulting in a surgery and potentially ending his lacrosse dreams. But Pete was tenacious. He told himself that he would get the surgery and work diligently to regain his level of strength and agility. His coaches and teammates tried to include him in many aspects of the team environment. Pete felt encouraged by his team when he was not able to play.

The physicality of the injury was difficult but so was the emotional toll on Peter. Being included in practices in various half-measures was not enough. Depressive thoughts began to creep into his mind like an unwanted houseguest. Pete blamed himself for his injury, asking himself what did I do wrong? Did I train too hard? Did I train incorrectly? Should I have not worn those new cleats?

The unanswerable questions and regrets continued to spiral for Peter, and he didn't feel comfortable admitting them to anyone. Though he didn't know it, Peter was falling into his first depressive episode.

He started to get irritable and sad. His identity felt shattered. Peter identified as a lacrosse player. That is all he ever wanted to be. He did not recognize a life beyond lacrosse. Without it, he spent many nights mourning his loss. He began to isolate from friends, family, and coaches. When his coaches and teammates reached out to him, Pete gave guarded answers and did not feel like he could be completely honest. He told them, "I am doing good. It sucks but I want to help the team out however I can."

He felt uncomfortable with expressing his emotions honestly and openly. Pete felt like a team should not be focused on the woes of one player, even though he felt his individual despair keenly. He sank into a type of cyclical questioning that always came back to the same thing: *Why would this happen when all I did was work so hard to achieve my goals?*

Pete did his best to work through the rehab and his major depressive episode. He returned the following season for his sophomore year. Pete stated to me later, that he was only 75% healthy upon his return. He worked as hard as he could in rehab, but he just needed more time to get back to his full physical potential. That was never something that he would admit to the coaches or to his team. Pete once again returned to the grind to the fullest of his ability, never wanting anyone to see that he was not completely okay.

To keep him motivated, his head coach tried an interesting strategy. He told Pete that he was at the bottom of the depth chart and needed to work his way back up. Though the intention was a good one – to motivate Peter to apply himself in practice and make sure he was really fit and physically healthy for games, it had a very unintended consequence. Pete hadn't shared his depressive symptoms with his coach. Those symptoms coupled with having to start at the bottom of the depth chart dealt another blow to his already fragile mood. Without meaning to, the coach's action communicated to

Peter that he wasn't good enough anymore. It was a punishment rather than a motivator.

Despite being back on the field, Peter's depression worsened and his physical performance on the field did as well. He lost focus and motivation. He was sad most of the time and continued to be emotionally guarded. Pete never reached out to his coaches or teammates for help. He was fearful of the consequences. What would the coach say? Would he get benched until he felt better? What if playing time improved his mood? Would it be fair to play if he hadn't earned it? Peter met the criteria for Major Depressive Disorder.

Pete is responsible for his own mood, but hopefully people around him would notice and say something. It really does take a village. I would encourage anyone who thinks a teammate is depressed to say something directly to that teammate and to the coach. I know it may be uncomfortable to have that conversation, but do it anyway. Mental health is part of being a team. We cannot escape that fact. There are a lot of emotions and stressful situations that occur with being an athlete. Coaches are not therapists, but they are usually connected to an on campus mental health service that can help. Today, Peter admits that he regrets not advocating for himself and at least starting this conversation.

ONE NIGHT DURING HIS SOPHOMORE YEAR, PETE was out drinking with a few of his teammates. He was not feeling connected or included. He went home a bit early feeling depressed with suicidal thoughts. Thankfully, he called his mom. His mom called one of Pete's friends to take him to the nearest emergency room. Pete was finally being honest about how depressed he was feeling. Unfortunately, he was not admitted but he and his parents did find a licensed clinical therapist whom he started sessions with immediately.

A quick note on emergency rooms. Some are better than others. Most are busy and the nurses and doctors are overwhelmed. A patient is admitted if he or she is deemed a threat to himself or herself or a threat to others. Suicide assessments are completed in a quick manner and clinical rapport is not established simply because the clinician does not have the time to do so. It's unlikely that a young adult will feel completely comfortable in such a setting with crowds of people, codes being called from overhead speakers, and the potential for police officers to walk by every few minutes. Added to the fact that there's little privacy between people next to you, it's not surprising that it's difficult to be open about suicidal ideations. Emergency Rooms can be scary places. However, it is still better to go than not. Whenever you believe that someone is at risk for suicide, call 911 or take them to the nearest emergency room.

So, what happened next? Peter began therapy with a well-qualified Cognitive Behavioral Therapist (CBT). He used his strong work ethic to get better, this time, emotionally. He engaged in the therapeutic relationship and used CBT tools to challenge his thinking process and thus change his mood. Peter had three strong automatic negative thoughts that needed to be challenged.

1. My life is over without lacrosse.

2. I don't have any friends at this school.

3. All of the efforts that my parents and I put into getting better at my sport were a complete waste of time.

Remember the Cognitive Distortions? Peter, with the help of his therapist, was able to identify that his first automatic negative thought *"My life is over without lacrosse"* was distorted in several ways. Peter was using **all or nothing thinking.** He was also using **magnification and mental filter** and **disqualifying the positives.** Peter also identified that he was **fortune telling.** He was able to come up with a thought to replace it. This was a process for him and did not happen in one or two sessions. With work, Peter came to understand that there is a whole world outside of lacrosse that is interesting and rewarding.

Peter identified that his second automatic negative thought, "I don't have any friends at this school." was mostly **mind reading** but he was also using **mental filter** and **disqualifying the positives.** He understood that it was difficult to connect with his teammates when he was not able to play. He simply was not spending a lot of time with them. Most of his day was taken up with classes and rehab.

Peter decided to transfer to a different school. He met new friends and found a love for the outdoors especially in the form of hiking. He started studying sports marketing and decided to play lacrosse at the club level. He was able to find joy again. He connected well with other students in his classes. He found a broader definition of what it means to be happy.

The third automatic negative thought, *"All of the efforts that my parents and I put into getting better at my sport was a complete waste of time"* was a challenging one for him to replace. He eventually came to accept that he only has so much control over life. Bad things happen and it was not his fault. He did not do anything to cause bad karma. He was not being punished. Pete was able to accept this new way of thinking, believing that what he can control is making the best of the situation and keeping a positive attitude.

Today, Peter is doing well. He is once again a loquacious, loud, and happy young man who is passionate about his friends, new girlfriend and his new puppy. He is looking forward to a career in sports marketing, wherever that may take him. He now has the cognitive and behavioral tools to overcome symptoms of depression if they return.

## Part 3: What Parents Can Do

1. Assess any depressive symptoms by asking your child about the symptoms outlined in The Basics section or by administering the Burns Depression Scale.

2. Be supportive and talk to your child about what he or she needs – remember, sometimes the simple act of listening without judgement can send the strongest message.

3. Reach out to the coach if you are feeling stuck and ask if they've observed similar concerning behaviors or if they've had conversations with your child about their performance or attitude on the field.

4. Set up an appointment for therapy for your athlete and ask him or her if they would like for you to attend a session– let your athlete know that you are also willing

to put in the work involved in therapy. It can be a game-changer for your child in helping forge open and honest communications about their symptoms.

# Substance Abuse

## Part 1: The Basics

The definition of addiction has changed over the years. It's actually a fascinating metamorphosis. In the early 1900s, addiction was seen as a moral failing. The first *DSM* diagnosis included addiction as part of the sociopathic or antisocial personality tendencies.

The second edition of the *Diagnostic and Statistical Manual* (*DSM II*) published in 1968, expanded on the original archaic definition. It saw alcohol as an issue once it caused impairment in the individual's life. It highlighted three types of drinking; Episodic Excessive Drinking, Habitual Excessive Drinking and Alcohol Addiction.

These definitions gradually morphed into "abuse" and "dependence," taking the illness completely out of the personality disorders category and creating a category of substance use disorders which was considered in the context of the disease model.

The *DSM III*, published in 1980, explained Alcohol Dependence using the following qualifiers:

- A need to use alcohol to function in everyday life
- Withdrawal symptoms
- Binging behaviors

- Unsuccessful attempts at decreasing alcohol use

- Experiencing blackouts

- Continued drinking despite negative consequences

- Increased tolerance

Fast forward to 2022, and with the latest addition of the *DSM-5-TR* (fifth edition, text revised), we have the creation of a new category: Substance-Related and Addictive Disorders.

Its explanations are detailed and specific and considers the wide range of possible addictions, from alcohol use to gambling; plus highlighting the need for more research on the identification of gaming addictions. The *DSM-V-TR* (Text Revision) also explains how the brain's neurological reward system is activated and rewired.

The latest research on brain pathways proves that diseases such as alcoholism are truly not our fault, and therefore *not* a moral failing on the part of the addict. It's true that people with addictive tendencies should practice self-awareness regarding their triggers, but this does not happen overnight. Addiction at any age or of any substance is so hard to kick because we are actually hardwired for the reward system in our brain. When activated, this reward system gives us such an intense feeling or high that we are psychologically and biologically compelled to repeat that feeling.

I often tell my clients they are not responsible for having this disease of addiction, but they are responsible for their recovery. There is evidence for a genetic pre-disposition for the disease. There are also environmental influences as we shall see. Together, these factors mix to create a cyclone of sadness, isolation, and shame.

## Part 2: The Case Study

Suzi was about 8 years old, gliding through the water doing the breaststroke faster than most adults swimming freestyle. The sun glittered off the chlorinated water like little jewels on an evening gown. Her tanned face showed a determined look behind her goggles, but her body moved with the ease and grace of an athlete.

As Suzi got older, she also discovered soccer and lacrosse. She excelled at all three sports and continued to play them through middle school. Suzi was a gifted athlete with a great group of friends. However, she was completely unaware of how the disease of addiction was about to wreak havoc in her life.

Suzi had her first drink when she was in the 7th grade. She and her friends spent most weekends partying at a friend's house. The parents were home, but not entirely aware of what was happening in their oversized club basement. However, they felt that the girls were safe because whatever was going on was in the comfort of their own home.

This partying continued for the next several years. Suzi vomited because of being drunk for the first time the summer before her freshman year of high school. She drank excessively but no one noticed. Suzi began blacking out and joking with her friends that she did not remember chunks of time. Her friends would laugh and did not really believe her because it never happened to them.

One night, Suzi got so drunk at a party that her friends locked her in a closet in order to contain her. She blacked out and threw up in her friend's mom's rain boots. She did not remember most of it but saw the evidence of her drunken state the next morning.

During her junior year, Suzi began to really piece together that her drinking was not normal, but she quickly dismissed it by using expert rationalization.

*I go to a really good private school, she thought.*

*My grades are good.*

*I am excelling at lacrosse.*

*I have never driven drunk.*

*I am a fun drunk. I have never been in a fight or argument.*

*My father is an alcoholic who is in recovery and his stories were so much worse.*

Suzi watched the show "Shameless." She took solace and pride in the fact that she was nowhere near the train wreck of the main character. So, what is an alcoholic? Was Suzi correct? Was there really no need for her to worry?

Suzi continued to drink throughout high school, binging mostly on the weekends and rationalizing how her drinking was not that bad. Her dad used to drink every day. She was only drinking on the weekends. She quickly reached a high tolerance. Her body never slowed down, she was never hungover, and she stopped throwing up after drinking too much. Suzie did, however, continue to black out on a regular basis.

By the way, blacking out is not the same as passing out. Passing out is losing consciousness and essentially sleeping. Blacking out is losing consciousness but walking around and talking as normal. That is scary! Your body is desperately trying to tell you that it is so impaired that your frontal lobe needs to go offline for a while. Your body is using all of its energy to keep your heart beating and your lungs pumping to keep you alive. It is full of so much toxicity that critical thinking takes a backseat to existence!

Despite all of this, Suzi received a scholarship to play division 1 lacrosse. However, at the same time, Suzi was also meeting all the criteria for Substance Use Disorder. She had a serious issue and needed help but was able to justify her actions because she was still playing well and functioning well. No one was the wiser. This disease can be insidious.

Suzi started college and, in the first month, appeared to be adapting well. However, in October, she tore her ACL. Her surgeon did not ask her about her alcohol use or history of addiction. As part of her treatment, he prescribed her ninety OxyContin pills for pain management. As a result, she began using oxy in addition to alcohol. The high she created was intense and she loved how it made her feel. The combination was dangerous but it gave her a better high and she ended up craving more. She began to use more in quantity and more often.

Surprisingly, no one noticed. Suzi hid it from others and because her teammates were also drinking, no one questioned Suzi's behavior. Another surprise (a very lucky one) was Suzi's lack of withdrawal symptoms from the OxyContin. It dissuaded her from asking for another refill. However, her drinking increased and was most likely the reason why she did not experience withdrawal. This combination can be deadly, and Suzi dodged a bullet.

In the beginning of the lacrosse season, Suzi could not travel because she was still recovering from ACL surgery. She stayed on campus each weekend while the team travelled and drank heavily with the other teammates left behind.

She came home for her first summer after college with a heavy rotation of physical therapy, drinking, and seeing her friends. She went back to school in the fall only to have it shut down due to the Covid-19 pandemic.This was another ingredient in the recipe for disaster.

The team stayed on campus and guess what they did? Drank. They drank on campus, and they went away for weekend trips and drank. Suzi remembers (not clearly) a weekend trip away at a friend's cabin. She got really intoxicated and was annoying a teammate. The teammate pushed her and she fell and hit her head on the footboard of the bed. Afterward, Suzi reported that she could not speak; she was dizzy and unsteady on her feet.

She had a concussion.

When the group returned to campus, Suzi made an appointment with the athletic trainer to assess the severity of her concussion. She did tell her coach what happened, but no specific punishment was given out. However, it was the first time that someone became aware that Suzi had an issue. Things quickly unraveled after this.

In December of her sophomore year, Suzi was asked to pick up a family member from the hospital. It wasn't until that moment, being alone in the car with that person that a flood of memories was triggered. Suzi hadn't been aware of it, but suddenly horrific flashbacks of abuse brought with it a tightness in her chest. She couldn't breathe, her hands were clammy, and she broke into a sweat. Suzi wasn't sure what was happening, but her memories felt strong and vivid.

Parents, be present with your child as much as possible. Notice any small changes in behavior or mood and inquire. In Suzi's case, she was not going to share anything with anyone until she finally imploded. After winter break, Suzi returned to school in January of 2021. She was desperately trying to ignore the flood of nightmarish memories threatening to suffocate her. One night, Suzi got drunk and told her teammates that she wanted to hurt herself. She had a very serious look on her face and her teammates took notice. To their credit, they encouraged Suzi to go to the hospital. She refused and started to run. She was drunk out of her mind, carelessly flinging suicidal statements into the air. Her teammates banded together and tackled her and dragged her into their car. Suzi fought and even attempted to strangle one of her dear friends who was trying to help. Thankfully, no one was hurt. The girls called the assistant coach and she in turn, called the police. Suzi was taken to the hospital by police, but they did not admit her.

Suzi met with the coaches the next day and tearfully told them everything. She told them that she was an alcoholic, and she told them that she had been abused. The coaches informed her parents immediately. She was hospitalized soon afterwards.

What would you have done as the head coach?

A coach reminded me one day that there is no preparing for this. Division 1 coaches in any sport do not receive adequate training in mental health. There is no precedent or play book for what to do if your player is suicidal or dealing with a substance abuse issue. Most colleges and universities do not have a therapist or psychologist assigned to the team.

Coaches are in the delicate position of knowing their players well but are not equipped to handle everything that could be thrown at them. When a player is struggling, it seems likely that he or she will reach out to one of the coaches. The onus is automatically put on the coaches to fix it. They wear many hats but the only one they are trained for is coaching.

The head coach in this case had Suzi sign a contract stating she would remain sober and attend mandatory therapy if she was to remain on the team. Her father remained closely involved and supported the contract. Suzi readily signed it and committed to her recovery.

February 8, 2021, was the beginning of her sobriety journey. The family contacted me and asked me to work with Suzi on how to remain in college without drinking, stay motivated to attend classes, and deal with the overwhelming trauma memories that now haunted every inch of her brain and body.

Suzi's road to recovery was very challenging. We realized that she previously drank to escape the trauma memories that lived under the surface of her awareness. The alcohol became its own problem as well. It is a progressive disease and a way to cover up other major issues like depression, anxiety or trauma. It begins as a maladaptive coping skill and evolves into something insidious. This was very true for Suzi.

She constantly dealt with deep feelings of inadequacy and hopelessness. She had several flashbacks per day that derailed her. Suzi worked diligently to get better but unfortunately, she had to leave the sport of lacrosse behind her. It had to take a back seat to her recovery, which required her full attention if she wanted to survive. She had one relapse and several more suicide attempts. She was hospitalized several times and eventually went to a long-term treatment program.

Her tremendous commitment paid off. Suzi embraced her recovery from alcohol. She realized that she could no longer use alcohol to manage her feelings. It was never a long term solution. She learned how to face her symptoms with healthy coping skills like cognitive behavioral techniques, physical exercise and sharing with friends. Suzi goes out with her friends but now she is the designated driver and she leaves situations that are heavily dominated by alcohol. She also learned how to speak kindly to herself.

The horrible memories of abuse were difficult to share. In addition to using CBT, we also used a great trauma technique called Eye Movement Desensitization and Reprocessing (EMDR). Today, Suzi's trauma symptoms are minimal. She became an ambassador for a national group that spreads awareness on college campuses about mental health issues. It was both a way to give back to her community and a way for her to connect with others who are also suffering. It is so meaningful to know that you are not isolated in your own anguish.

The work that we did together was meaningful to both of us. It was based on trust. Suzi graduated from college and is thriving mentally and physically. She has over three years clean and sober.

I could not be prouder of her.


## Part 3: What Parents Can Do

1. Monitor your child's alcohol use. Acknowledge that even if they are still under the legal drinking age, your child will most likely experiment with alcohol. If or when they do drink, remember that if they're talking to you about it this means there's trust in your relationship.

2. Ask your child about other drugs he or she has tried and be willing to listen about their experience.

3. Set up an appointment with a licensed substance abuse therapist if you suspect that their drinking or drug use may be excessive.

4. Use a non-judgmental approach – the priority is keeping your child healthy, not punishing or condemning their behavior.

5. Be aware of your own thoughts of denial. There is usually a family history since this disease is genetically based. However, in rare instances, it may not be present. Do not use this lack of family history to assume that your child does not have a substance use disorder.

6. Do not use shame to try to change your child's behavior. Instead, accept it and wrap them with support. You may even want to stop drinking in order to create a safe environment. Get rid of the alcohol in the house. Lock up prescription drugs.

7. Attend family support groups like Al-Anon. If your child is in an outpatient program, attend the family night. Ask questions. Get involved.

8. Examine your own alcohol use. Is it excessive? Have you ever experienced negative consequences due to drinking?

9. Explore Alcoholics Anonymous meetings for your athlete. It is an excellent support system and they are attended by a wide age range.

# Anxiety

## Part 1: The Basics

There are many different types of anxiety disorders, including phobias and panic disorder. The most well known may be Generalized Anxiety Disorder (GAD). According to the *DSM-5-TR*, GAD is excessive apprehension and worry about any number of things in a person's life. The symptoms are present for most days and extend over a period of at least six months. Other symptoms include:

- Feeling on edge
- Feeling tired
- Finding it hard to concentrate
- Feeling irritable
- Having muscle tension
- Having trouble sleeping

Managing anxiety disorders is a process just like getting into better physical shape or learning a new skill. There are many factors that can affect one's anxiety level; lack of sleep, poor diet, studying for a big exam. Unmanaged anxiety can sometimes lead to panic attacks. It's important to recognize anxiety triggers and to understand that stress and anxiety felt in one area of a person's life can often create ripple effects that impact other areas such as interpersonal relationships, academic performance, and overall physical wellbeing.

## Part 2: The Case Study

Liz was a sophomore in college playing Division 1 lacrosse when she landed in my office during winter break. Her primary reason for seeking therapy was anxiety. Liz's parents were strong advocates of mental health and have seen their own therapists over the years. They encouraged Liz to reach out to a licensed clinician to get the help she needed. Liz wanted help with three issues; the first two regarded her relationships with two different people and the third issue was the run test for her lacrosse program. The run test was a specific series of sprints that had to be finished in a specified time frame. It was very difficult for most of the team to complete.

Over a few sessions, we processed each one in great detail. She quickly felt better about her relationship anxieties. However, the run test haunted her. Her anxiety was so strong that she was fearful that it would hamper her physical ability to actually complete the test. Liz's run test consisted of thirteen full 100-yard sprints, running up-field in twenty seconds and running back in forty seconds. There were no breaks allowed.

Her biggest fear was that she would fail. With this as her starting point, often her thoughts led her down a negative spiral.

*"I will fail the run test,"* she thought, *"and then I will lose my starting position. It will be awful and embarrassing, and I will never be able to get back to the starters."*

Liz and I worked together to find some coping skills that she could readily use. The first one regarded her thinking. She was given the handout on Cognitive Distortions and she found examples for some of them. The ones that resonated with her the most were **fortune telling, mind reading, all or nothing thinking and emotional reasoning.** Then, she was taught the triple column technique (using the same template found in the first chapter). Liz was able to start talking back to her negative thoughts with reasonable and believable replacement thoughts.

For example, one of her strongest negative thoughts was *"I will fail the run test."* She identified that she was using the distortions, **fortune telling and emotional reasoning.** Liz was also able to identify that she had passed the run test the year before as a freshman and this year she was in better physical condition after having one college season under her belt. Her replacement thought was *"I have prepared to the best of my ability."*

She rated her statement as 100% believable. It was what she could control. She could not tell herself that she *will* pass it. That would be **fortune telling** again. She prepared well and did all she could to improve her chances of success. The believability for the automatic negative thought dropped down to 30% when she reassessed. She began to feel less upset and anxious.

As an additional coping skill, we added practice with visualization and some meditation. I asked Liz to stand on the end line of the field, close her eyes and breathe deeply. Inhale for a count of seven, and exhale for a count of eight. Being able to relax her mind and body while standing in the spot where she experienced the most stress helped her perform better on testing day.

To practice visualization, Liz imagined herself completing the run test successfully. Allowing her to see it in her mind, was a very powerful step in translating it to a real experience. This was helpful to her, and she returned to school and passed the run test. We discussed how every athlete goes through periods of increased stress, but it's important to remember that every athlete has a different threshold for optimum performance. Some athletes do very well when the pressure is on, some crack under pressure, and most fall somewhere in the middle. It is up to the athlete to determine his or her ideal level of stress and then recreate it as best as possible.

A few weeks later, Liz requested another session because her anxiety spiked again. She had some difficulty in explaining why her anxiety had spiked, and she was increasingly frustrated by it and the uncomfortable symptoms she experienced because of it. In cases like this, I reminded her, it's important to remember that this is a process. Likely, Liz had experienced anxiety for most of her life, stemming primarily from automatic negative thinking. It wasn't something that would or could disappear completely after just three sessions.

Liz eventually determined that she was anxious about doing well on an exam in one of her classes. That anxiety spilled over to the lacrosse field. This time, Liz and I used the Reset Strategy as I like to call it. If she felt herself getting anxious during a game or practice, she came out (she was the draw girl so this was easy to implement) and took some deep breaths. She identified what she needed to improve on (if anything) and visualized herself doing it. Then she went back in to take another draw. This strategy also worked well for her.

Liz did a great job for several more weeks and then called

again for a session. This time she knew exactly why her anxiety spiked. Her coach, seemingly randomly, took Liz out of the starting draw girl position and put in the back up. Liz was livid, confused, and worried. She was flooded with negative self-talk, specifically *"what did I do wrong?"* She was doing very well and winning most of her draws, so being pulled out of the starting position spawned a pool of *"what ifs."*

What if I am not good?

What if the coaches like her better?

What if my anxiety gets the best of me and I lose all of my draws?

The coaches told her that they wanted to give the backup a chance to improve. Liz and her backup began to alternate taking the draw. While rationally, Liz understood the coach's reasoning for moving her out of a starting position, that didn't stop the fears she held that she somehow was being told that she wasn't good enough.

Liz had used the triple column technique on her own, but it was not working for her this time. Instead, we used the evidence technique, another visualization technique and some mindfulness.

To try the evidence technique, we examined the concrete evidence around Liz's stressor – being removed from starting position. We used statistics on how many draws she has won or lost. Liz, being the excellent draw girl that she was, had these stats on hand! She shared that she wins over 60% of the time. She also knew that she was in the top 5% in the nation for draws, which was astounding. The simple act of reading these stats out loud, seemed to improve her confidence. It impressed me, too.

We also tried a technique which required Liz to personify her anxiety as a way to talk back to it more effectively. Liz named her anxiety, Carol (sorry to all of the Carols out there). Liz gave "Carol" long curly black hair that was out of control. She visualized her facial features as large and off-putting. "Carol" was big in stature but not muscular or strong. Liz drew a picture of Carol and began to talk to her. Liz told Carol to move out of her head. Carol was banished to a nearby street corner with Liz's angry words following her.

*"I have worked really hard to be where I am,"* Liz told her anxiety, *"And you are not going to take it from me!"*

She immediately felt calm. We introduced one more coping skill during that session: mindfulness. Liz was to practice being mindful and present the next time she steps onto the field. I encouraged her to notice the little things: how the grass or turf feels under her shoes, how the stick felt in her hand, and how the ball settled into her stick. I asked her to tune in to her stance to determine if any adjustments needed to be made once she was ready to draw.

Liz practiced these coping skills over the next few weeks of her season. She performed very well, and her anxiety remained low. She was calm and focused on lacrosse, which, in turn, carried over to her performance in the classroom.

We had four more sessions to monitor her progress and deal with any other issues that came up for her, like anxiety about taking the LSATs. Liz has since graduated with a degree from a wonderful university and is now thriving in law school. She is an amazing young woman, and I cherished every minute of our time together.

## Part 3: What Parents Can Do

1. Administer a mood survey to assess the anxiety level. Excessive anxiety is going to negatively affect overall functioning.

2. Introduce the cognitive distortions and the triple column technique. Have an open conversation with your athlete about any distortions they may be using; remind them that their emotions are valid, but there are healthy ways of dealing with anxiety that will take time and practice.

3. Introduce a simple breathing technique to manage anxiety in the moment; start with a six-count inhale and a seven-count exhale. Remind your athlete that when they are feeling stressed, they can allow themselves the time to prioritize their mental health.

4. If the anxiety level has not improved in two weeks, find a therapist for your athlete who specializes in strategies for coping with anxiety.

# Injury and Illness

## Part 1: The Basics

In a study by Pierpoint et al in 2019, 700 injuries were reported in girls high school lacrosse during the 2008/2009 season through the 2013/2014 season. This number was out of 481,687 "athlete exposures" (AE) or each instance when a student athlete was in a practice or game. Similarly, 1027 injuries out of 287,856 AEs were reported by the NCAA for women's lacrosse. Concussions were reported as the most common diagnosis. The numbers for boys lacrosse was 1,407 out of 662,960 AEs in high school and 1,882 out of 390,029 athlete exposures for college. In a study by D'Alonzo et al in 2021, 4.90 injuries were reported per 1,000 AEs in men's college lacrosse. These injuries occurred mostly in games. The most reported injuries were concussions (8.0%), ankle sprains (7.7%) and hamstring tears (6.9%).

Injuries lead to time off the field and sometimes, away from your teammates. It is a shock for the player to experience such an abrupt change of schedule and social interaction. Whether their injury is a result of time on the field or related to unforeseen circumstances, learning to deal with them and managing the social and emotional impacts are a big part of ensuring your athlete's success and meaningful recovery.

## Part 2: The Case Study

In early February of 2022, my son called me and my husband and told us that he was having trouble breathing and experiencing lower back pain. Like most athletes, he does not complain about injury or illness because if he does, then most likely he would not get to play. They ALL want to play.

We were alarmed and took him to a clinic where the doctor performed a chest x-ray. After that, things spiraled out of control quickly.

The chest x-ray revealed that my son had many small lesions on his lungs. The doctor stated that she did not know what it was. The next day, my husband took him to see a pulmonologist. The pulmonologist believed that my son had pneumonia and prescribed steroids, a round of antibiotics and Advil three times per day. There was some improvement for a few days but within a week, the difficulty breathing and the pain in his lower back returned.

I took him to the emergency room where the ER doctors ran more tests and told us that his lung issues were a result of Covid-19, although he tested negative. When we pressed them for more details, the nurse quickly left the room and told us that we were free to go.

The next day my husband took our son to the pulmonologist once again and his diagnostic team performed a chest CT on site. It revealed pulmonary nodules and effusion throughout his lungs which indicated a metastatic disease like cancer.

Lung cancer, testicular cancer, and septic emboli were the clinical hypotheses. We were immediately sent to the ER at a local hospital for further tests. We were seen through triage where the nurse seemed genuinely empathetic to our situation. She told us that she would say a prayer. I remember holding back tears as we followed another nurse to a room in the emergency department. My son walked ahead of me. He calmly greeted the nurses with a confident hello and a smile. He was nineteen years old and facing a cancer diagnosis.

Who is this kid?

How did he get the grace and emotional strength to handle this?

None of us are prepared for this. Our nurse and the attending physician prepared him for several different scans. I did my best to keep things light. My husband stayed in the waiting area with the locals, as only one visitor was allowed due to the Covid restrictions at the time. We both wanted to be with him, but we were too tired to argue with the hospital staff at that point.

After several hours and constant texts to my husband with updates, the attending and the chief of the emergency department came back to talk to us. My son and I looked at each other with concern as we watched them make a beeline to our room from the long dark hallway. They told us that cancer was not yet ruled out, but tests were coming back normal. We exhaled a few sighs of relief.

We were released from the ED and recommended to see a thoracic surgeon at another local hospital. A day or two later, my husband took our son for the initial consultation where again the diagnosis of cancer was addressed as a possibility. It was a scary and serious conversation. It was the first time in this process that a doctor took the time to talk about cancer as the most likely cause of my son's issues.

The next step was to confirm it. My son had a needle lung biopsy on February 22, 2022, with the chief thoracic surgeon. My husband had his turn this time, waiting nearby as a needle pierced my son's chest gathering tissue from these villainous nodules that had taken over his lungs.

After three tortuous days, we were informed on February 25, 2022, that it was *not* cancer. The surgeon's diagnosis was one of a rule out. Instead, my son was diagnosed with sarcoidosis, an inflammatory disease marked by the formation of granulomas in the lungs, lymph nodes, or even the heart. Some people can live without issues for most of their lives, but there is no known cure. The three of us met in the doctor's office to discuss what this meant. Sarcoidosis is not easily diagnosed. There is no confirming test. It is a diagnosis that is given once everything else has been ruled out.

The surgeon's recommendation was to let it be. Sarcoidosis can be managed, and he was very hopeful that due to my son's age and being an athlete, this will not give him many issues in the future. The surgeon specifically told us to avoid the sarcoidosis clinic at Hopkins because they will *"treat him like a lab rat and write a paper on him."*

My husband and I have an uncanny way of being on the same page when it comes to big decisions. We left the surgeon's office and called Hopkins.

We met with a specialist from the Johns Hopkins Hospital Sarcoidosis clinic in March, 2022. It was a zoom meeting with the doctor, me, my husband and our son. After our interview, she immediately let us know that she suspected it was not sarcoidosis. However, she was willing to work with us to find out what it actually was. Up to this point, my son kept a positive mindset. He was dealing with each stressor as it came, and he was remaining in the present with his thoughts. This news, however, sent him into an emotional tailspin. I worked with him to avoid the distortion of **fortune-telling.** Naturally, my son was predicting that more negative things would occur and *"this will never end."* These thoughts were understandable but not helpful. I encouraged him to practice a simple breathing technique (6 count inhale and a 7 count exhale) and stay focused on only the here and now. I also encouraged him to focus on the positives and avoid using **mental filter.** Yes, there were negatives, but also positives. He is young and healthy and he was being treated by the best doctors.

So, onward we went. The tests performed thus far, did not reveal the true identity of this mysterious illness. Hopkins ordered every test on the face of the Earth. My son also had to wear a heart monitor for a short period of time. Cardiac functions came back as normal; however, my son's liver functions were abnormal and reaching a concerning level. The doctor called me and my husband on Saturday, March 12. She was concerned that he could go into liver failure and wanted him hospitalized immediately. We agreed (although I admit that I was initially reluctant) and my son was admitted late that afternoon. The staff at Hopkins could not have been kinder.

He was placed in a special room with its own ventilation system because tuberculosis or other communicable diseases had not been ruled out. They asked that my husband and I wear PPEs (personal protective equipment) if we were not going to stay in the room permanently. We said no thank you and they left us alone. My son was scheduled for a bronchoscopy to biopsy the lesions/opacities on his lungs and to biopsy a lymph node. At the same time, another test called a flow cytometry would be performed to look for blood cancers. These tests would require him to be under general anesthesia. We spent several days in the hospital waiting for the bronchoscopy and flow cytometry to be scheduled.

My son was in the hospital when his team played a big rival game that weekend. My husband set up his laptop so the three of us could watch it together from the hospital bed. Later, my son's freshman roommates snuck in to see him. The staff made an exception, only asking that the motley crew did not come in all at once. This was helpful. My son was feeling separated from the team and the visit lifted his mood and gave him more energy to get through the next few days.

Unfortunately, my son kept getting bumped back because other patients who were sicker than he was obtained the priority for the test. We were understanding, but it was tough because he had a standing NPO (In Latin, this is *nil per os* or "nothing by mouth") order as he awaited the test. This means, the kid was starving for several days with only an IV and occasional crackers and small round plastic cups of apple juice with a label that tears off the top. These snacks were the meager reward of knowing that the test was not going to be performed in the next twelve hours because a sicker patient took his spot. So be it.

One morning at 3:00 a.m., I finally lost my temper when a phlebotomist came in for the twentieth time to take what seemed like a second gallon of blood from my son. He was weak and tired. I asked the phlebotomist if there was a new test ordered. He was not aware of anything new. I asked if taking more blood was really necessary. He told me he had to follow through with his orders. I raised my voice and told him that there would be no more blood drawn from my son. I told him that he had all the blood needed and to run the damn tests from the gallon that he already had. The phlebotomist said in a cracked voice, "I am just the phlebotomist." He promptly left.

My son told me the next day that another phlebotomist came into his room and looked sheepishly around. My son looked at her quizzically. She asked, "Is your mama here?" We had a good laugh.

My son was released on March 15, because he was stable, and the bronchoscopy could not be scheduled. The next day, the hospital called and said they could perform the surgical procedure. So, back up we went.

The bronchoscopy and flow cytometry were both successful. We brought him home that evening, awaiting the results.

We returned my son to his lacrosse team the next day. He was happy to be back with them. He took it easy but attended classes and practice. The normalcy was good for his body and mind even though he was still not allowed to engage in physical activity.

My husband and I aggressively watched the online healthcare portal for test results to come in, all the while discussing the medical hypotheses that were still valid. There was one hypothesis that had not been ruled out. My son had strep throat early in January. He had been treated for it via a local clinic.

That following Saturday, while we watched my son's college team compete on our home field, the specialist called and reported (much to our collective relief) that the results of all tests were negative for cancer.

Strep was found in his lymph node. We started to complete each other's sentences as our medical nightmare slowly unraveled before our eyes.

Within minutes, the doctor, myself, my husband and my younger son discussed the diagnosis that had stolen six months and a lacrosse season of my son's life. Strep. The Z-Pak that my son had taken in January never fully killed the strep bacteria. The bacteria got worse, giving my son symptoms. The steroid taper he was prescribed in February allowed the strep to grow systemically, forming bilateral necrotizing granulomas on his lungs.

We had a decision to make. The doctor wanted to prescribe Keflex, part of the penicillin family. As a child, my son had been deemed allergic to penicillin. He can receive IV antibiotics in the hospital, or we can give him Keflex at home and watch him like a corgi watches a carrot. My younger son said, matter-of-factly, "why don't you just get an EpiPen?"

Huh, 17-year-old son who knows it all – okay, good idea.

After the game (I don't even remember who won) I talked to my son about the plan. A fellow teammate saw the look on his face and quickly came over to join our conversation. Riley, a brilliant young man with an even better character, gave my son reassurance that it would be better to receive the Keflex at home. We did just that. I watched him for 24 hours with an EpiPen in my hand. Riley, by the way, is now finishing up his first year in medical school at the time of writing this book.

Finally, after weeks of uncertainty, our medical ordeal drew to a close. My son had a few follow ups with a Hopkins liver specialist to monitor his liver enzymes. For several weeks, his liver enzymes decreased but at the end of May, there was an unexplained increase. The liver specialist recommended a liver biopsy which revealed normal results. There was no fibrosis or any abnormalities. We still do not know why his enzymes were elevated but it was not linked to any negative symptomatology. My son continues to follow up with the specialist for liver fibrose scans.

My son put in significant effort to get back into excellent physical shape. He engaged in strength training several times a week with his team's strength coach. He ran frequently and practiced every day. He sought out fellow teammates to play 3-on-3; met with his shooting coach and asked his goalie friends to practice with him. He was determined. He is one of the most focused people I have ever met. He wanted to play the sport he loves but he also wanted to contribute to the team as a leader on and off the field.

He started the Fall of 2022 strong and in great shape. He was playing well and then my husband got a phone call from the team trainer. My son got hit with a shot during practice and it broke his jaw. He was immediately taken to the hospital, a place he was all too familiar with. My husband and I met him there. His trainer was sitting by the side of his hospital bed.

I will be honest. I nearly passed out. The blood and facial swelling were a bit more than I had the stomach for. He had surgery on October 5, which, thankfully, went off without complication. The trauma facial surgeon inserted two metal plates in his face and wired him shut for 6-8 weeks. We eventually returned him to his two roommates with wire cutters. I was uneasy as I had to explain to them that if my son starts choking, they would have to cut the wires for him. I was leaving my son's health in the hands of two college kids. Seriously? Luckily there were no emergencies. Once he recovered and the wires were removed, my son got back to work yet again. He eased back into lifting and running and practicing. He was excited to play for the Spring season. But a few weeks later, we received another call. My son got a concussion during practice. The trainer put him on the concussion protocol. Everything went smoothly. Then, he rolled his ankle in practice and was out with a high ankle sprain. He missed his entire Sophomore year after missing his entire Freshman year.

This chapter is a ludicrous example of injury and illness, and I hope your player never has this experience, but I also know many of you have. My son did receive two extra years of eligibility, but it is at a significant cost.

**Part 3: What Parents Can Do**

1. Stay Positive: Give your player positive feedback. Let him/her know that he/she is strong and can overcome this. Let him/her know that he/she has the support and love of his/her friends and family. Remind your athlete that he/she is not alone. Have him/her reach out to others who have gone through the same thing. Let your athlete know that going through adversity is a powerful learning experience that initiates growth and maturity.

2. Present options when challenges or setbacks occur: Not every player is going to choose to stay in their

sport after such adversity. Let your athlete know that it is okay to transfer, to find new interests, and to take a step back. Let him/her know that it is okay to never play Division 1 again. Let him/her know that it is okay to take a short break. Taking a week off can be a great option to focus on one's mental health and get back into a mental mindset that is more conducive for competing. It is not quitting, and it is not weak. It is making the best decision based on his or her emotional and physical needs. Have a conversation with your player about how he or she is feeling about it and weigh the pros and cons. Do not utilize pressure. Make the decision with them and not for them.

3. Continue emotional assessments: Periodically assess your player for symptoms of depression and anxiety. The symptoms are presented in the chapters above for you to refer to. You can also give your player a mood survey so he or she does not have to verbalize feelings or thoughts. There is no shame in getting depressed or worried about what you are experiencing. Normalize it for your player by saying, "it is normal to be depressed or anxious about what you are going through, I am just curious about where you are at this moment."

# Graduation

"*Every single day we put our lives into it and then it's over.*" Leaving college and lacrosse behind is a sad and difficult transition. Whatever sport you played in college, you have most likely been playing it since a young age. How does an athlete cope with graduation?

Liam, a recent college graduate and division 1 lacrosse player, was kind enough to speak with me about it. He shared that one of the most shocking losses is the competition. He has been competitive since childhood, and he needed to find another way to channel this need. Liam focused on excelling at work, and he joined sports like pickle ball and a running group through the One Love Foundation. Liam shared that his life didn't feel complete without a sport and a sense of competing. He found a sense of purpose in other ways like working toward earning a promotion.

Liam shared it was initially hard to get back into the gym. It was fun when he lifted with his team, and he enjoyed the camaraderie, and the work involved. Now, it was no longer a requirement, and it was harder to stay motivated when it was no longer with his team. Now, working out became a decision. Liam tried to trick his brain into saying he had to exercise every morning. Mentally doing this before work, got him on the right track for the day. The mental toughness that his coaches instilled in him helped him adapt.

Liam was upset to graduate. It is a loss, but he felt that his time was coming to an end, and he emotionally and logistically prepared for it. He secured summer internships in his last three years of college. The first internship was helpful for him to get his second one at a bigger firm. He stayed at the second internship for two years and locked down a job before graduation. The next stage of his life was planned out and ready to go. He had a place to live, roommates and a good job.

In minor ways graduation was reviving for Liam. He experienced some physical and emotional burn out, from playing his sport at a high level for five years. His body was beat up and the emotional stress was consistent. During a normal season, Liam recalled that going to bed the night before a game was hard. He was nervous and excited. He wanted to perform well for his team and put additional pressure on himself to not let them down. Most players on his team did not sleep well before a game.

But after graduation, Liam noticed that he felt less stressed overall, and his sleep had improved. I asked Liam how he adapted socially. He shared that of course, his friend group got smaller. Now he sees his roommates most of the time instead of his fifty closest friends who he saw continuously at practices. He looked forward to seeing his team in the locker room and hanging out after practice, but after college he spent more time with a smaller group of friends. Liam found himself alone more often, but had plans to go to happy hours on Thursdays to stay connected to his teammates.

Another transition for Liam was having to be more independent with logistical responsibilities. He no longer has the team administration to schedule doctors' appointments and travel plans. Liam sheepishly shared that he relied more on his mom for some of these things now but felt that as he got more comfortable with adult responsibilities that he would take over more of the initiative. I am sure most of these players will do the same!

He recently went on a trip with his girlfriend, and he had to plan it. It was strange to do so on his own, but learning how was a challenge he readily accepted. Liam found booking the flight and renting a car to be easy. He has also figured out how to navigate the DC metro. Liam enjoyed learning these new things and discovered he liked the freedom.

Still, Liam admitted, going back to his university to watch a game was emotional because he had a strong desire to play. It was bittersweet, but he was able to work through these emotions by reminding himself of what he has already accomplished.

Overall, Liam was happy and at peace with how his division 1 lacrosse career went for him. He didn't have any regrets and he felt hopeful about the next steps in his future.

My last question for Liam was this:

*Me: What advice would you give to the recent grads?*

*Liam: Explore new areas. Take the risk to move away. Try something new. Live somewhere new. Hang out with friends more in college when you can. Continue working out. It is a huge benefit, physically and mentally. Take your job seriously and make it your sport. Work hard to find what you like to do. You don't want to dread it. Don't settle. Also, finding an internship while in college really helps prepare you for a job after graduation.*

# References

Burns, D.D. (1999). *The Feeling Good Handbook* 2nd edition. Plume.

Burns, D.D. (2020). *Feeling Great: The Revolutionary New Treatment for Depression and Anxiety.* Bridge City Books, an Imprint of PESI Publishing, Inc.

D'Alonzo, B. et al. (2021). Epidemiology of Injuries in National Collegiate Athletic Association Men's Lacrosse: 2014-2015 Through 2018-2019. *Journal of Athletic Training.* July; 56(7), 758-765. doi: 10.4085/1062-6050-612-20.

Pierpoint, L.A., et al. (2019). The First Decade of Web-Based Sports Injury Surveillance: Descriptive Epidemiology of Injuries in US High School Boys' Lacrosse (2008-2009 Through 2013-2014) and National Collegiate Athletic Association Men's Lacrosse (2004-2005 Through 2013-2014). *Journal of Athletic Training.* Jan; 54(1), 30-41. doi:10.4085/1062-6050-200-17.

Pierpoint, L.A. et al. (2019). The First Decade of Web-Based Sports Injury Surveillance: Descriptive Epidemiology of Injuries in US High School Boys' Lacrosse (2008-2009 Through 2013-2014) and National Collegiate Athletic Association Men's Lacrosse (2004-2005 Through 2013-2014). *Journal of Athletic Training.* Jan; 54(1): 42-54. doi: 10.4085/1062-6050-200-17.

American Psychiatric Association (2024). *Diagnostic and statistical manual of mental disorders* (5th. ed., text rev., p.183, 251-255, 553-561). Arlington, VA: American Psychiatric Association.

American Psychiatric Association (1968). *Diagnostic and statistical manual of mental disorders* (2nd. ed., p.45); American Psychiatric Association.

American Psychiatric Association (1980). *Diagnostic and statistical manual of mental disorders* (3rd ed., p.170); American Psychiatric Association.

Beck Institute: *Cognitive Behavioral Therapy.* Retrieved from https://beck-institute.org/about/dr-aaron-t-beck/#earlylife

Wikipedia, (2025, May 17). *David D. Burns.* Retrieved from https://en.wikipedia.org/wiki/David_D._Burns#:~:text=Burns,-Article&text=Article-,David%20D.,Treatment%20for%20Depression%20and%20Anxiety.&text=Burns%20popularized%20Albert%20Ellis's,her%20teenage%20son%20with%20depression.

Wikipedia, (2025, June 2). *Operant Conditioning.* Retrieved from https://en.wikipedia.org/wiki/Operant_conditioning

Ibraheem, R. et al (2024, September 25). *Classical Conditioning.* StatPearls Publishing Company, LLC. Retrieved from https://www.ncbi.nlm.nih.gov/books/NBK470326/

Dillon, R.F. and Dillon, A.D. (2024). *Little Albert Study.* Retrieved from https://www.ebsco.com/research-starters/psychology/little-albert-study#:~:text=The%20Little%20Albert%20study%2C%20conducted,of%20its%20results%20over%20time.&text=By:%20Dillon%2C%20Ronna%20F.,PhD%20%7C%20Dillon%2C%20Amber%20D.

National Collegiate Athletic Association (2024, April 1). *Estimated Probability of Competing in College Athletics.* Retrieved from https://www.ncaa.org/sports/2015/3/2/estimated-probability-of-competing-in-college-athletics.aspx

Schilling, V. (Spring 2021, vol 22; 1). *The Creator's Game: Native People Created Lacrosse Yet Now Strive to Play the Sport in International Arenas.* American Indian, Magazine of Smithsonian's National Museum of the American Indian. Retrieved from https://www.americanindianmagazine.org/story/the-creators-game

www.ingramcontent.com/pod-product-compliance
Lightning Source LLC
Chambersburg PA
CBHW071953100426
42736CB00043B/3161